DATE DUE

Death

Coping With the Pain

by Eileen Kuehn

Consultant:
Roderick W. Franks, MA, LSW
Licensed Psychologist
Hennepin County Family Court Services
Minneapolis, Minnesota

Grief and Loss

LifeMatters
an imprint of Capstone Press
Mankato, Minnesota

LifeMatters Books are published by Capstone Press
PO Box 669 • 151 Good Counsel Drive • Mankato, Minnesota 56002
http://www.capstone-press.com

Printed in the United States of America

Library of Congress Cataloging-in-Publication Data
Kuehn, Eileen.
      Death: coping with the pain / by Eileen Kuehn.
           p.   cm. — (Grief and loss series)
      Includes bibliographical references and index.
      ISBN 0-7368-0745-4
      1. Grief in adolescence—Juvenile literature. 2. Bereavement in adolescence—Juvenile literature. 3. Loss (Psychology) in adolescence—Juvenile literature. 4. Teenagers and death—Juvenile literature. [1. Grief. 2. Death.] I. Title. II. Grief and loss.
      BF724.3.G73 K84 2001
      155.9´37—dc21
                                            00-010421
                                          CIP

Summary: Defines death and how it may affect teens. Describes death as part of life and ways in which people react to death. Provides ideas for dealing with death, as well as how to move beyond it and return to a normal life. Also gives tips on helping a friend experiencing someones death.

Staff Credits
Charles Pederson, editor; Adam Lazar, designer; Kim Danger, photo researcher

Photo Credits
Cover: UPmagazine/©Tim Yoon
International Stock/©Gerard Fritz, 18
©2001 The Munch Museum/The Munch-Ellingsen Group/Artists Rights Society (ARS), New York, 20
Photo Network/©Mary Messenger, 26; ©D&I MacDonald, 29; ©Myrleen Cate, 49
Photri, Inc., 11/©Les Riess, 21; ©Skjold, 31
Unicorn/©Jeff Greenberg, 36, 39; ©Karen Holsinger Mullen, 44
Uniphoto Picture Agency, 9, 41/©Llewellyn, 16; ©Jackson Smith, 23; ©Greg Crisp, 55
UPmagazine/©Tim Yoon, 59

A 0 9 8 7 6 5 4 3 2 1

Table of Contents

- Death is a natural part of life. Today, medical technology and healthier lifestyles help many people live longer.

- Knowing what to expect when a person dies may help survivors prepare for the death of a loved one.

- After death, a funeral is held to honor the life of the person who died. The body is often buried or cremated.

- In different parts of the world, people treat death in different ways. Cultures and religions have their own traditions in observing death.

Death

Chapter 1

Death: Completing the Life Cycle

Death is a natural part of life. Every living thing on earth is born, lives its life, and dies. Plants, animals, and humans go through that same life cycle. Often in nature, death comes suddenly. Among humans, death may be sudden, too. However, in places including North America, many people live long and die from diseases of old age.

Death once was more accepted as a natural process. People couldn't always go to a hospital, so they often died at home with their family around them. More people died at earlier ages. There was a higher rate of death among young children and young mothers.

Fast Fact

Around 1900, the annual death rate was about 17 per 1,000 of the U.S. population. In the late 1990s, the annual death rate was fewer than 8 per 1,000 of the U.S. population.

Marvin, Age 17

"My best friend's dad died of a disease. It seems like he took a long time to finally die. The hospital kept him breathing with a machine. If this were 50 years ago, his dad would have been considered dead long before. My friend was pretty angry that they didn't just let his dad die normally."

The father of Marvin's friend died in a hospital. He was kept alive with a machine. That's not unusual these days. Medical technologies and healthier lifestyles help extend life. New treatments for illness can keep many people alive longer. Death is unfamiliar to most people and may seem far away. People often don't want to think about death. Not wanting to think about death or pretending nothing is wrong when someone dies is called denial.

What to Expect When a Person Dies

Knowing what to expect when a person dies may help you prepare for the death. A person near death may look physically different. The dying person may become thin. The face may lose its normal appearance. Sometimes the face looks puffy or swollen. The dying person may not be able to get out of bed. The person might lose the use of the arms and legs.

Burial practices from hundreds of years ago suggest that many people thought the dead were in a special kind of sleep.

As a person dies, the body's functions begin to shut down. Sometimes this happens all at once, sometimes it happens more slowly. Years ago, people were considered dead when their heart and breathing stopped. Because of today's technology, death is harder to define. It still includes the lack of heartbeat and breathing. It also includes lack of physical activity, reflexes, and brain activity.

Death may happen as a result of a long or a short illness. Or it may happen suddenly because of an accident or war. When someone kills himself or herself, that is called suicide. It's another kind of sudden death.

Preparation of the Body

After death, a body often is prepared for interment. This is the act of burying a body in a grave or tomb. Sometimes a person or the person's family may have decided on cremation. This is burning the body in a very hot fire.

Whether buried or cremated, the body is usually taken to a funeral home. If the body is to be interred, the funeral staff prepares it for burial. Interment is burying a body in the ground. Sometimes the body is dressed in a favorite outfit of the person who has died. The hair and face are treated with cosmetics to resemble how the person looked when alive.

The body may be embalmed. This means the blood and other fluids are replaced with fluids that help preserve the body. Sometimes the body is bathed and wrapped in a plain shroud. This is a white cotton sheet. The preparation of the body often depends on the religious or cultural practices of the person who died.

After the body is prepared for interment, it's laid in a casket or coffin. These are boxes or chests in which the body is placed and carried to be buried. Sometimes the casket is open before or during the funeral. A funeral is the special ceremony that allows family and friends to say good-bye. Sometimes the casket is closed. The deceased may have made this choice before death, or the family may decide. It also depends on the condition of the body. For example, the body of a person who died in a fire wouldn't be in an open casket.

If the body is cremated, the funeral staff doesn't prepare the body for viewing. It's taken instead to a special place called a crematorium to be burned. The clean, white ashes are placed in an urn that the family receives. An urn may look something like a vase. Often it's placed on a table or altar at the funeral. A picture of the person may be placed next to the urn.

After the funeral, the ashes may be treated in different ways. They may be buried in the earth. Sometimes they're tossed into the air over a favorite place of the deceased. They may be taken out to sea, scattered over a lake, or spread on a mountaintop. Sometimes the ashes are put in a vault at a cemetery. Sometimes the family keeps the urn and ashes in a special place.

Sarah, Age 14

Sarah was a gifted musician who studied piano for 10 years. When her grandmother died, Sarah went to her piano and began playing a variety of music. Some pieces sounded like hymns. One sounded like the noise of a huge family dinner. Another sounded like her grandmother picking flowers in the garden she loved so much.

Sarah played and played until the different pieces sounded like one. "I want to play this at Gram's funeral," she told her mother. "I can say good-bye to her this way."

A Final Good-Bye

In most cultures, funerals serve an important purpose. They are an opportunity for people to accept the death of a loved one. This is one of the first steps in the grieving process.

Funerals can be a way for friends, family, and others to say good-bye to the person who has died. There are many ways to do this. Sarah decided to play music at her grandmother's funeral. People may sing, read from a book, or tell stories about the person's life. Others express their love and respect through a final kiss or tender touch. Sometimes a family member or close friend puts a note or memento in the casket to be buried with their loved one. A memento is a small gift or token that has a special meaning. After the funeral, the body is interred in a cemetery.

A wake may be held before a funeral. At a wake, family and friends gather to remember special moments and celebrate the dead person's life. There may be singing, music, readings from holy books, prayers, and food. Sometimes jokes and other humorous comments about the loved one are shared.

Sometimes a person is honored by a funeral procession through the streets of town. This may resemble a parade. The coffin containing the body is placed in a hearse—a special car or a wagon pulled by horses. A marching band may play. People may join in the procession. Some processions are small, some are much larger. The funeral procession of John Kennedy, who was shot and killed while serving as U.S. president, was very large.

Aleesha, Age 13

Aleesha had cancer. Aleesha loved life even though she couldn't do many things other teens did. Every day was new and wonderful to her. She knew she wouldn't live much longer. She wanted to plan her own funeral. She wanted it to be happy—like a birthday party. She wanted balloons, streamers, music, food, and even a birthday cake. "I want it to be in our backyard," she said. "I'll be up there enjoying it with everyone."

Sometimes the person who dies plans his or her own funeral in advance. In North America, people often treat death as a sad occasion. Many people are uncomfortable with Aleesha's idea that death should be treated like a party. However, some of the seriousness surrounding death is changing. More and more people want to celebrate the life of their loved one with joy. This isn't disrespectful, but rather a tribute to the life of the deceased.

At a Glance

Different cultures have different images of death. The phoenix is one. This is a bird that dies in a fire but rises from the ashes to live again. You may sometimes hear people talking about death as being a bright light.

Death and Dying in Different Cultures

People in different parts of the world have different beliefs about death and dying. Funeral customs vary. Religious traditions deal with death in different ways.

For example, some Hawaiians believe death is with them no matter where they go or what they do. When someone dies, all the friends and relatives come. First there's a wailing procession. Then the body is buried. After that there's a big feast. The ceremony always includes children. They learn early that death is part of life.

Many Alaskan native peoples die when they feel it's time. The dying person calls together relatives and friends. There are final good-byes, prayers, and singing. Often the person dies within hours or a day after the gathering.

When a follower of Islam dies, family members and friends often surround him or her. When the person dies, the women make a noise called ululation. It's a high-pitched wail that can mean either great joy or great sadness. The person is bathed, wrapped in a shroud, and placed in a simple wood casket. Nothing else is done to the body. The male members of the family immediately carry the casket to the graveyard. Islamic tradition requires that the person be buried, never cremated, within a day of death.

Death

More people in Western countries buy the Tibetan *Book of the Dead* than any other work except the Bible. The *Book of the Dead* contains certain Eastern beliefs on how to die well.

Jewish people share the tradition of gathering at the bedside of the dying person. Members of the community may come, too, so the dying person is never alone. The burial service is simple, as is the coffin. People visit a grieving Jewish family after a funeral. This is called sitting shiva and may last for several days. A Jewish religious leader reads special prayers. Refreshments may be served as people talk and remember the dead person.

Points to Consider

- Think of someone who has died. How do you feel about the person's death?

- What would it be like to attend the funeral of someone close to you? How would you feel about it?

- Would you prefer to plan your own funeral or have someone else take care of it after you die? Explain.

○ Sometimes the death of a loved one is expected, especially after a long illness. This gives survivors time to prepare for the death. They can say good-bye to the loved one.

○ A hospice service can help a make a dying person's last days easier.

○ The feelings a person experiences when a loved one dies can range from intense pain to numbness to relief.

○ Edvard Munch is an artist who tried to express the feelings people go through after the death of a loved one.

○ Generally, a survivor goes through three types of feelings when a loved one dies. These are bereavement, mourning, and grief.

Death

Chapter 2

What Happens to Survivors After a Death?

Preparing for the Death of a Loved One

When a death is expected because of a long illness, survivors have time to prepare. The time may help them learn to accept the death. They have more time to deal with their feelings, say "I love you," or say good-bye. It's harder to be prepared for a sudden death. Accepting death as part of life is one way to prepare for sudden death or longer illness.

Some people say it's a special gift to share the final days of their loved one's life. This is one reason some families care for a terminally ill family member at home. Being terminally ill is having an illness that can only end in death.

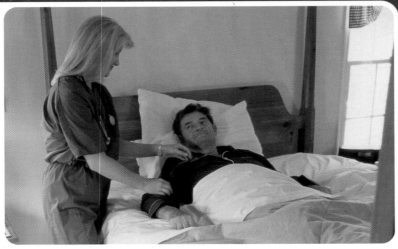

Mary and Tom, Ages 14 and 17

Mary and Tom were close to their grandmother Ida. Then seven years ago, she developed an illness from which they knew she would die. At first Ida only had problems with her memory. As her illness got worse, Ida could no longer walk. She couldn't feed herself or recognize people she should have known well.

Finally, Ida died. Mary and Tom were happy that she wasn't suffering any longer. They were sad, but they felt lucky to have shared in their grandmother's final days.

Hospice

When terminally ill people need special help, a hospice service may be set up. A hospice is a place where dying people are cared for. A hospice may be in a hospital or nursing home, but more often it's set up in the home. Many people want to have familiar objects and people around them. Trained nurses and home health aides come into the home to help care for the dying person.

It's normal to forget things after a loss. People have been known to forget even simple things such as their own phone number.

Usually, the dying person needs a hospital bed and other special equipment. The person may need oxygen and painkilling drugs. The goal is to keep the person comfortable while the body is shutting down.

Regular meals aren't served in a hospice. Only snacks and beverages are given to the dying person if food is requested. This is often difficult for family members to understand. But when a human body is dying, the vital organs such as the heart, brain, or lungs are shutting down. The body no longer needs or desires the foods that the dying person used to like.

Living Will

How to care for a dying person may be written out in a legal document. This legal document is called a living will. If a living will has been signed, usually no extra measures are taken to keep the person alive. This means no artificial devices will be used to prolong breathing. No tubes will be used to give the dying person food.

A Rush of Feelings

The feelings that a person experiences when a loved one dies are unlike any other emotions. The feelings may be deep and painful and touch every part of the body. Or a person may feel numb, guilty, or even relieved. Sometimes a person feels all these emotions at the same time. It can be confusing.

When someone we love dies, we first may feel like we're frozen in place. Many people ask themselves some of these questions:

- "How could he do this to me?"

- "How could this happen?"

- "How can I stand the pain?"

- "Why can't I feel anything?"

- "Could I have done anything about it?"

- "What will I do now that she's gone?"

"When my grandfather was dying, my mother decided to move him into a hospice. At first, I was mad at her for that. Later, I realized it was a way to let my grandfather die with dignity. It gave us a chance to say good-bye to each other."—Debbie, age 15

"I almost didn't go the funeral of Mr. Hakes, my math teacher. He was like a father to me. I couldn't stand the thought of saying good-bye to him. But I also couldn't stand not saying good-bye either. So I went. It was terrible, but I'll survive."—Trey, age 16

Edvard Munch's "Death in the Sick Chamber"

Writers, singers, dancers, and other artists have tried throughout history to express the feelings that death brings. The Norwegian artist Edvard Munch is one example. He painted "Death in the Sick Chamber" to show the death of his 14-year-old sister. The body language of the people in the painting shows the different ways people may act when someone dies. Body language is communication without words through body positions, gestures, or facial expressions.

Look at the body language of the people in the painting on the next page. No one faces the others. Each is alone in grief. There's no talking, sharing, touching, or comforting. Each is withdrawn. Here's what you'll see, starting from the left:

A young man is braced against the wall. His back is toward the other people in the room. The young woman facing front is staring at nothing. Her back is to a young man looking at the deathbed. Neither pays attention to the other. They also pay no attention to the girl in front of them. Her head is bowed and her hands folded together.

An older man, standing by the bed, has his head bowed. His hands are clasped as if in prayer. A woman seated on a chair at the bed has no face. Her body is shaped like a question mark, perhaps asking: "Why did someone so young have to die?" Another woman holds the back of the seated woman's chair. Her body is bent over in a posture of great loss.

Each figure seems to be at a loss about what to do next. None seems ready to leave the room. But that's what they must do. Outside the room, they must pick up their life and go on.

Bereavement

At the death of someone we love, we first experience the feelings of bereavement. It can also be called grieving. It includes the feelings of shock or sadness at death. It happens to those who loved the person who died. Bereavement or grieving includes a feeling of loss of control. Death is a fact. It's best when we can accept it. Grieving is described more in Chapter 3.

Mourning

After the first shock of death passes, people move to the next type of emotion, mourning. This is when survivors try to accept the death of a loved one.

People look for answers about how to go on with life without the loved one. A funeral often helps make the death a reality. It likely will be a sad time. But it's also the time when healing can begin.

Sometimes parents try to keep teens from being involved in a funeral. They want to spare their teen the pain of attending. However, many counselors and experts on dying believe young people benefit from being involved in a funeral.

Mourning also includes the way religions or cultures observe special traditions during the funeral period. For example, in some societies, survivors sometimes wore only black clothing for months after a death. They didn't go to parties or other events. This told the world they had lost a loved one. It was a signal that people in mourning were to be treated with great respect and understanding.

Grief

The third type of emotion people feel after the death of a loved one is grief. It's a feeling of sorrow or deep loss. This is how people learn to handle sadness and live without the loved one.

Grief happens after any major loss. The death of a loved one changes a person's life. In periods of grief, the challenge is to learn new ways to heal after a loss.

As we learn and relearn ways to go on with life, we cope with the loss. The feeling of loss is still there, but successful coping helps the feeling fade over time.

Death

Points to Consider

- How do you think someone in a hospice feels? What feelings do you think the family has?

- Do you think an artist can express emotions about death better than most people? Why or why not?

- What are some ways to deal with the pain of a loved one dying?

- The grieving process is different for every person. There's no right or wrong way to go through the grieving process. Dealing with grief can take time, maybe even years.

- A sudden death can make the process more difficult. You might be shocked or stunned and have many questions about why the death happened.

- The grieving process usually consists of three phases: avoidance, confrontation, and accommodation. Each phase has its own emotions.

- Grieving can help you grow and mature as a person.

Chapter 3

How We Grieve

The grieving process can't be hurried. Grief can last as long as two years or more. It can come and go without warning for many years—sometimes throughout life. There's no right way to grieve because everyone is different.

Sometimes the way the death happens makes a difference in the way a person grieves. There's pain in both sudden and anticipated death. Violent deaths sometimes are the hardest kind to face. A sudden or violent death may cause guilt, anger, and self-blame. You may need a longer time for these feelings to fade.

James, Age 15

James feels it was his fault that his six-year-old brother, Billy, killed himself. James knew the gun was kept in the back of his father's desk drawer. James tortures himself with dozens of things he thinks he should have done or said. Now it's too late. "I might as well find the gun and kill myself, too," he thinks.

Sudden Death

A sudden death may shock and stun family and friends. They have many questions about why the death happened. They had no time to prepare for the death or say good-bye. When not prepared for the death, a person may blame himself or herself. Guilt and blame can make it harder.

Experts say it's healthy to express your feelings. When you name an emotion, it's often easier to face. But it's not emotionally healthy to continue to blame yourself. Instead, work to get on with the healing to be found in helpful grieving.

Grieving Phases

Experts on grieving say the process has several phases. Each phase involves a separate kind of reaction to the loss of a loved one. The three phases are avoidance, confrontation, and accommodation.

Some people find it helps to talk with others about the person who has died. Sharing the pain of death can help the healing to begin. Others prefer not to talk about death. They find it easier to talk about ordinary things in life. In either case—talking or not talking about death—that choice needs to be respected by friends and family.

It's important that grieving people allow themselves to work through all the phases. It's also important to realize that a phase lasts until it's finished. A phase may take more time for some people, less for others. Time isn't something to worry about. Working through the phases simply takes as long as it takes.

Avoidance

Avoidance is the first phase of grieving. It's when you try to deny that the death happened. In some ways, it's healthy. Avoidance is the body's way of helping to deal with death a little at a time. You might have several reactions at this phase of your grieving.

- **Shock.** You may be confused, dazed, and numb. You may not understand what has happened. You might feel disorganized and unable to make sense of anything.

- **Denial.** You may feel disbelief that the death happened. You want to avoid the reality of the death. You may feel that you'll see the person doing some everyday thing. At this time, it's normal to want to know why the death occurred, especially if it was sudden.

- **Numbness.** Some people withdraw and act like robots without feeling. Some people call this emotional anesthesia. This means losing the ability to feel emotions.

Teen Talk

"After my best friend died, I just pretended she was away on vacation. I told myself she was coming back to school in the fall. It let me cope with the pain a little bit at a time."—Kristeen, age 16

"I didn't want to talk to anyone about my mother's death for months after it happened. Finally, one day I asked my dad if he missed her as much as I did. We both cried for a long time. Then we had a good talk about my mother. I felt a lot better."
—George, age 14

Lorenzo, Age 15

Lorenzo's mother died in a car accident. Lorenzo felt nothing. He couldn't even cry.

"What's the matter with me?" he thought. "Mom's dead, and I can't even cry. I feel dead, too." Two days after the funeral Lorenzo still hadn't cried a single tear. Then, walking in the garden, he saw the rosebush his mother had been so proud of. Suddenly, great, gulping sobs shook his body. He fell down beside the bush and continued to sob into the grass. Finally, the sobs ended. Now he felt everything: pain, sadness, shock, disbelief, anger, guilt. Lorenzo felt tired, too. But at least he could feel again.

Death

Confrontation

The second phase of grieving is confrontation. This is when you accept death, and you feel the loss most sharply. During this phase, you accept that the loved one is gone. But you still may want to reach out to the loved one who has died. For example, you may want to talk with your dead mother. Or you might start to call your dead friend to play basketball with you. It's then you realize these people are gone.

You may have outbursts of anger, tears, screaming, overwhelming sadness, or feelings of being abandoned. You may experience many other confusing reactions at moments when you least expect them.

The confrontation phase of grieving may happen at the funeral. It may come during a private time at home. It may occur at another time.

Confrontation can help you handle the reality of death. Although painful, each confrontation of death is a small step in coping with your grief.

Accommodation

The third phase of grieving is a gradual acceptance of the death. You notice fewer instances of the sharp, confrontational grief. This is the accommodation phase, when you slowly learn to live with the loss of that loved one. At this time, grief slowly becomes less painful. Little by little, you feel able to cope better in your life.

Guilt is a common feeling at this phase. You may feel guilty because you're living while your loved one is dead. You may feel guilty that you're having fun or being happy without your loved one. However, with these feelings comes the gradual relearning that you can live with the sadness and hurt.

The accommodation phase takes the most time to work through while grieving. Some people may need years.

Death

Growing as a Person

Grieving can help you grow as a person. Working through the grieving process can give you a better understanding of yourself. You may learn to make wiser choices or to value life more. As you put time and energy into self-examination, you can begin to realize how important each day is.

Points to Consider

- If a loved one died suddenly, what feelings do you think you might have? Explain.

- Why do you think grieving is such hard work?

- A leading expert on death says that as we understand more about death, we learn more about life. Do you agree? Why or why not?

Chapter Overview

- Healthy grieving helps heal the sadness of the mind, body, and soul.

- Healthy grieving can be done through grief work. This includes giving yourself time to think about the death of a loved one.

- Grief work activities are helpful in working through grief.

- There are many ways to get help during the grieving process. If you decide to seek the help of a trained counselor, there are some things to consider.

- Many organizations exist to help young people deal with grief.

Death

Healing After a Death

Healthy Grieving

Healthy grieving is good. When a loved one dies, grieving is helpful in healing the sadness in your mind, body, and soul.

At a Glance

Sometimes, parents or friends seem to hover over you after a death. If you feel you need some space, ask them in a kind way to back off. Remember, they're only trying to protect you from pain. But experiencing the pain is necessary to work through the grieving process.

Paula, Age 16

Paula didn't plan to become pregnant, but slowly she began to love the baby growing inside her. She knew it was a boy and named him Alexander. She began to make plans to care for Alex at home. She'd finish school and get a job.

Then during labor, Alex died. Paula was stunned. She wanted to hold Alex, sing to him, and kiss him. Paula's parents tried to arrange for a quick cremation of Alex. They wanted to protect Paula from more pain. However, the funeral director insisted that Paula should be part of the decision. Paula thanked the funeral director for letting her make her own decisions.

Paula cried a lot while she decided. The next day, Paula told the funeral director she wanted to bury Alex, not cremate him. She wanted a small casket that looked warm and soft. She wanted to see Alex at the funeral home and attend his funeral and burial.

On the day of the funeral, Paula went to the funeral home two hours early. She asked to be left alone in the room where Alex lay in the casket. When she came out, dried tears streaked her face, but she looked peaceful.

When the funeral director went into the room, he saw that Alex's blankets had been moved. Pinned inside was a note that said simply, "I love you. God will take care of you now."

Paula found helpful ways to grieve her loss. She said good-bye at the funeral home and shared her love with Alex once more. She needed to work on her grief for a while. But she accepted Alex's death and was ready to rebuild her life.

Grief Work

Healthy grieving includes doing grief work. This is an effort to deal with the sadness of a loss. The only one who can do your grief work is you. No one else can make your decisions or feel the pain necessary to recover from losing a loved one. However, it's sometimes helpful to do your grief work with a friend or family member.

During grief work, you may need private time and a private place to think about your loved one. Making a contract, writing lists, anchoring joy, and mind-mapping are examples of grief work.

Make a Contract

Make a contract with yourself to do grief work every day for two or three weeks after the death. Spend 15 minutes to an hour per day to let out all your feelings about the death. You may do this alone or with a friend or family member.

Write Lists

Write headings in a journal or on a sheet of paper. For example, you might write *Sad, Afraid,* and *Angry.* Under each heading, write lists of whatever comes to mind. For example: "I'm sad that you went away." "I'm afraid to be alone." "I'm angry we can't do things together anymore."

When you've finished all your lists, take them to a private spot. Read the lists out loud and let the wind carry the words away and set them free.

Anchor Joy

Recall events in your life when you were happy, contented, or having fun. In your mind, revisit one of those events. Feel again what it felt like to be there. Take a deep breath and touch something such as a finger on your hand. As you touch the finger, imagine that you're putting all those good feelings into it. Holding something in place like this is called anchoring.

You can visit other events with other fingers. Each time you feel sad, touch a finger to remind you that joy hasn't gone for good.

Death

"My friend Jack is nuts about running. Every day he takes a long run after school. One time I asked him why he does it. He said it's his way of working out his anger. He started doing it right after his pet cat died. He said he felt kind of silly, but he really loved that cat. I guess deep feelings aren't only for people's death."—Frank, age 17

Do Mind-Mapping

You may be familiar with mind-mapping from school. In grief work, it's another way to help release your feelings.

In the middle of a piece of paper, write the name of the person you're grieving and circle it. Then draw a line in any direction. At the end of the line, draw another circle. Write the first word that comes to mind about the name in the center circle. For example, you might write *funny, black hair,* or *trip to museum*. Keep adding circles with words in them for 10 or 15 minutes. Doing this can help you remember the person as he or she was.

Other Grief Work

Other helpful ways to do grief work can include the following:

- Find safe ways and safe places to act out your feelings: Pound or scream into a pillow. Have a fit of temper on your bed.

- Go for a long walk or run.

- Make noise: Howl, laugh, cry, yell, or sing.

- Dance, paint, or draw your feelings.

Did You Know?

Some American Indians had a special way of releasing grief for the loss of a loved one. They went to the woods or a private place. There, they dug a hole in the ground near a tree or bush. They poured all of their feelings into the hole. When everything was poured out, they covered the hole. They thanked the tree for listening and Mother Earth for receiving their grief. Then they returned to their regular activities with a lighter heart. Sometimes, they would repeat the procedure as more layers of grief came up.

- Think quietly in a special place.

- Listen to music.

- Read.

- Write letters in a journal to your loved one. Get everything off your chest.

- Do deeds of kindness for others.

- Create a personal grief ritual. Burn candles, set up photos of the deceased, or read a poem or story that the person liked.

- Have fun with other people.

How to Ask for Help

When you're in pain, you may need a trained professional to help you deal with it. Don't be afraid to ask for help.

Death

If you want to talk with a trained counselor, ask parents, school counselors, teachers, religious leaders, or other trusted adults. Do you know someone who goes to a counselor? Ask if the person respects and likes the counselor. If so, ask for the counselor's name and telephone number and call the counselor. Your parents or guardian can help you in calling.

- Ask the person to tell you about himself or herself.

- Does the person work with teens?

- Ask yourself how you feel when you have your first talk with the person. If you're overly anxious, you can decide if you want to keep looking.

- Does the person accept you for who you are? Does she or he really listen to you?

Organizations That Can Help

Many organizations can help teens deal with their grief when a loved one dies. These organizations offer private advice and can refer you to other helpful sources. As a starting place, check the For More Information section starting on page 60. Check out other resources advertised in your school or community. These may include support groups and teen help lines.

The Internet also is an excellent source of information. Refer to the list of helpful Internet sites starting on page 60. Always be careful about sharing personal information if you correspond with someone on the Internet.

Points to Consider

- How could you express anger or sadness about a death? How might that be helpful?

- What do you think about the American Indian grieving tradition?

- Do you think it's a good idea to interview a counselor before you decide to begin working with him or her? Explain.

- Grief can be compared to building a sand castle that a wave washes away. The wave may destroy the castle, but it can be built up again.

- Letting go of a relationship with someone who has died is an important step in healing. Letting go doesn't mean forgetting the person. It means thinking of him or her in a different way.

- Over time, unreleased grief can cause serious diseases and depression.

- When a loved one dies, the pattern of life changes. Nothing seems to work as it used to. We must relearn life and begin to do things in new ways.

- As people work through their grief, they sometimes become stronger and wiser. They learn the value of living each day to its fullest.

Moving Beyond Grief

A Story About Grief

Imagine yourself as having built a sand castle. You worked hard to make it beautiful. You were proud of it. Grief is like what happens when a wave knocks the castle down and washes it away. You couldn't stop the wave from destroying your castle. You were sad and angry.

You couldn't do anything about the wave or the ruined sand castle. So you decided to build another sand castle. It would be even better than the original sand castle. You now know that you always can build another castle, in spite of the waves.

How to Go On

This story can show what happens in the grieving process. It also can show you how to learn to go on with your life. Think of the sand castle as your life before the death of your loved one. The wave is like death. The sadness you feel over the loss of your castle is a form of grieving.

Taking steps to rebuild your sand castle might be compared to the grieving process. Grieving is something you do. It's active. You let go of the past. In this case, that's thoughts about the first sand castle. You go on with your life, or build another sand castle.

Grieving is like building the new sand castle. While building it, you may continue to think about the castle you had. You may wish you could have the old castle back. But you can't, so you keep building the new one. As your new castle takes form, you think less and less about the old castle.

By concentrating on building the new castle, you move on with your life. You let go of the past. This is how we learn to live life without the person who has died.

Death

Brian, Age 14

Every day, Brian looked forward to breakfast. He loved breakfast because it was a special family event. Sometimes his father made his surprise omelet. You never knew what would be in it unless you peeked into the refrigerator first. The rule was to "take time to enjoy breakfast." It started the day for Brian and his little brothers.

One day, Brian came home from school to hear the awful news. His father had been killed when the building he was working on had collapsed. Brian, his brothers, and his mother mechanically lived through the days and weeks following the funeral. Breakfast wasn't fun anymore. Often, it was simply a matter of grabbing some food and hurrying off to school or work. No one felt like eating anyway.

"Our family's broken," Brian told his track coach. "Nothing works anymore. We used to do everything together. Now we hardly know each other."

"When something's broken, you have to find ways to fix it," the coach said. "Your family won't be exactly what it was. But you can begin to learn new ways to make your family come together again."

Relearning Life

We often take many things for granted. For example, what we eat, our time with our family, what we do in school or with friends. All of our activities and relationships are tied together. When a loved one dies, this pattern breaks. Suddenly everything seems different.

Learning to live without a loved one is a slow process. It may take years. You must take many small steps to move forward in rebuilding your life. You must find new ways to live without your loved one. That's why experts on grieving call this relearning or rebuilding your life.

Choosing to Live Again

One decision is necessary at this time. You must choose to live again. This means getting beyond your grief. It's still there, but it no longer rules your life. You begin doing things in new ways.

Brian is beginning his relearning. He recognizes that his life pattern is broken and seeks help from his coach.

Jon, Age 13

It's been over a year since Jon's mother died. Yet Jon insists that everything remain just as it was before she died. His mother's things are just where she left them. Jon even insists that they set a place for his mother at the table.

When Jon's father and two younger sisters tell him it's time to stop this, Jon has a temper tantrum. "I don't see why anything has to change," he said.

Letting Go

Letting go in grieving means changing your relationship with a loved one who has died. Letting go is hard to do. It may feel like you didn't really love the person who died. Jon's mother can no longer play an active role in his life. He still has memories of her. However, it may not help Jon to think of his mother as an active part of his day-to-day life.

Jon's refusal to let go of the past is an unhealthy form of grieving. On one level, Jon knows his mother isn't coming back. On another level, he denies that the death happened. Denial may protect you from pain for a while, but accomodation must replace denial.

When Jon can move more into healthy grieving, he'll accept that his mother is dead. He'll no longer need to set a place for her. He'll quit trying to put his father and sisters at a distance with his tantrums.

At a Glance

Here are some ways you can tell if a friend may be acting out grief in an unhelpful manner:

- Gets worse grades or has other problems at school
- Begins using alcohol or other drugs
- Does reckless things; for example, drives too fast
- Eats too much or too little
- Is angry and confrontational
- Fights with friends or family members
- Feels guilty for the death
- Has difficulty concentrating
- Seems depressed or withdrawn

Letting go doesn't mean forgetting about your loved one. It means giving permission to yourself to live without him or her. Say good-bye and fill your heart with loving memories.

In helpful grieving, you may need to let go again and again in different ways. It's the most important thing you can do to begin your healing.

Unhelpful Grieving

If you continue to grieve in unhelpful ways, the body and mind can become sick. When too many bad feelings are stuffed into the body, it may overreact. Sometimes it may react with a stomachache. You may get a headache or develop skin problems. Other painful reactions may occur. If the grief isn't released at all, over time the body may develop a serious disease. Watch for behaviors that may warn that a person has slipped into unhelpful grieving.

Depression

Unreleased grief can make a person severely depressed. Depression is a mood disorder that includes deep feelings of sadness or hopelessness. Signs of depression can include:

- Lack of energy

- Inability to concentrate

- Fears and guilt

- Not wanting to get out of bed

- Lack of interest in personal appearance

- No interest in anything

- Forgetfulness

- Continuous crying

- Eating disorders

- Withdrawal from other people

Teen Talk

"When my friend Karla died, I couldn't leave my room for a week. I wouldn't eat or sleep. I just stayed there and cried. Then, one night I dreamed about Karla. She was smiling at me. Somehow, I felt she was okay and in a good place. The next day, I started to do things again."—Julie, age 14

"First, my mom died of cancer. Then my brother died in a motorcycle accident. When that happened, my world ended. But my aunts, brothers, and sisters helped each other through the grieving process. It's been two years. I still miss my mom and brother, but I think they'd like our new ways of doing things." —Monika, age 16

Being depressed makes it extremely difficult to deal with grief. The good news is that depression usually can be treated with counseling, medicine, or both. If you or someone you know is depressed, ask a trusted adult for help. That adult can help you find a doctor or counselor.

Your New Life

During the avoidance phase of grieving, you might not think about rebuilding your life. It's too much just trying to cope with the death. But when you begin to accept the loss, the work of rebuilding or relearning life can really begin.

Relearning doesn't mean being done with grieving. It does mean making new choices about your life. Relearning can begin as you answer some questions:

- What's different now because my loved one is dead?

- Am I doing things that my loved one used to do? Is this appropriate behavior for me?

- What do I most enjoy doing?

- What activities have meaning in my life?

- Am I willing to take some risks and try new things?

- What do I hope to be doing in 5 years? 10 years?

Many people say that as grief becomes less, they can see themselves as stronger and wiser. They have relearned the value of living every day. They have grown beyond their grief to find new purpose and meaning in their life.

Points to Consider

- What do you think of the story about the sand castle? Does it make sense to compare grief to building a sand castle? Explain.

- How would you let go of a relationship with a loved one who died?

- If you've experienced the death of someone close, how has the family of the deceased changed?

- How could you help someone who's grieving in an unhealthy way?

Chapter Overview

○ As a friend, you can help someone through the grieving process.

○ There are many ways to help a friend who's grieving. Being an active listener is one of the best ways.

○ Give a grieving friend a journal to write feelings in. You also could help him or her to join a teen support group. These are good ways to help a friend grieve.

Death

Chapter 6

How to Help a Friend Who Is Grieving

Only the person who has lost a loved one can do the hard work of grieving. But a loving family and friends can help.

It may be hard to be a friend to someone who's grieving. People who grieve often feel confused, powerless, and helpless. They may feel separated from other people. They may tend to push friends away. For example, you may try to be a friend to someone who's grieving. However, that person may rudely tell you to mind your own business. Being a friend to someone who's grieving takes courage. It also requires understanding and patience.

Teen Talk

"The pain will change. It did for me. You must choose to stay in the light. Get rid of the dark thoughts."—Shandra, age 14

"Grief is as hard to sort out as egg yolks scrambled into egg whites. Everything is all mixed up together."—Maria, age 16

Minh and Claris, Age 15

Minh and Claris were best friends since second grade. Recently, Minh's 17-year-old brother Sam committed suicide. Minh felt Sam's death was her fault. After the funeral, Minh wouldn't leave her room. She refused to talk with anyone.

Claris's heart broke as she thought about what had happened. Claris had loved Sam like a big brother. She wasn't sure what to say to Minh. She decided to talk with her school counselor about it first. The counselor suggested that Claris cope with her own grief first. She told Claris, "Minh may not be able to talk about it yet. But in time she'll probably want to see you. Helping Minh may help you with your own grief." The counselor had some suggestions for Claris.

Helping a Grieving Friend

Here are some of the things the counselor told Claris:

- It's important to understand that a grieving friend hurts a great deal.

- Often, a grieving friend isn't aware of being rude.

- Grief numbs feelings.

- Your friend may resent you at first.

Death

- No one can grieve for another person. But being there may help.

- Leave your friend alone when that's appropriate.

- Never give advice unless your friend asks for it.

- If your friend begins to act in an unhealthy manner, talk with parents, religious leaders, teachers, or other trusted adults. You aren't betraying your friend by discussing these challenges.

- Listen actively.

- Be available to the grieving friend whenever needed.

- Try to help your friend take small steps into the future.

- Take your own recovery from grief one day at a time.

- The grief gets better after a while. Try to stay optimistic until it does.

Minh and Claris, Age 15

Claris went over to Minh's house after school every day. "I'm here if you want to talk," she'd say. At first Minh yelled at Claris to "just go away."

"I'll be back tomorrow," Claris said. "We don't have to talk. I'm your friend, and I just want to be with you."

One day, Claris brought over a video she and Minh planned to rent before the suicide. "Do you want to watch that video with me?" Claris asked through the door.

Claris heard Minh unlock her door. Claris and Minh hugged each other. They cried and cried but didn't talk. Finally, Minh said, "We better watch that video, or you'll get charged for bringing it back late."

In the days that followed, Claris and Minh began talking about Sam and themselves. They discussed how it wasn't Minh's fault that Sam killed himself. Slowly, Minh began to understand she had to go on with her life. "But I'm still angry with him for dying," she said.

"So am I," said Claris.

One day, Minh decided she wanted to go for a walk. "I'm tired of being stuck in this stuffy room. Let's do something fun for a change!"

Claris was glad that she thought about talking with her school counselor before she visited Minh. Remembering the counselor's suggestions helped her get through the first terrible days.

A good gift for a grieving friend is a blank book. Tell your friend it's a place to write his or her feelings. Explain that journals are private and that the writing doesn't have to be perfect. No one else reads a private journal. These suggestions may help a grieving friend begin writing in the journal:

- Set aside time when you won't be interrupted.

- Write about whatever you're feeling.

- You may want to write down your dreams.

- If you can't get started, try beginning a sentence with: "I'm remembering . . ." Do this whenever you get stuck.

- Put your pen on the blank page. For 10 or 15 minutes, write anything you think of. Don't read it until the time is past. Just keep writing without lifting the pen from the page. This can help you get in touch with hidden feelings.

How to Listen Actively

A good way to help a friend through the grieving process is to be an active listener. An active listener does more than just hear someone talk. An active listener pays attention to what's being said. Two skills help you be an active listener:

- Having empathy

- Being a word detective

When you have empathy, you can feel what someone else is feeling. Remember a feeling you've had that's something like what your friend is telling you about. Imagine yourself having your friend's feeling. Empathy can help you be more understanding.

Did You Know?

Support groups and organizations can help families grieving the death of a loved one. These groups can:

- Give teens a safe place to express feelings

- Be a source for finding new friends

- Help young people understand grief-related feelings such as anger and denial

- Help young people with their grief work

- Improve family relationships

A word detective hunts for clues about what someone is really feeling. There are three ways to do this.

- **Listen closely to what your friend is saying.** Concentrate completely. Don't think about what you will say next, just think about what the person is saying.

- **Listen to what your friend *isn't* saying.** Your friend may talk around the subject he or she is really concerned about.

- **Listen for the words your friend uses.** These words can translate into feelings. For example, your friend may say: "I have nothing to live for." Your friend may mean: "Maybe things would be better if I killed myself, too."

Support Groups Can Help

You may want to suggest that your friend join a teen support group. The people in a support group share similar grief feelings. For example, teens in an alcohol support group have all experienced the effects of alcohol. Teens in a grief support group have lost a loved one. Talking about things in a group often helps with the healing. Offer to go to the first meeting with your grieving friend if necessary.

A Special Friend

It takes a special friend to help another person through the grieving process. It can be difficult at times. It may stretch the friendship to the breaking point. It also can make the friendship stronger.

Helping a friend who's grieving can help you grow as a person. Grief work comes from the heart. It's a pathway to your own greater joy and well-being.

Points to Consider

- Do you find it difficult to talk with a grieving friend? Explain.

- Do you consider yourself an active listener? Why or why not?

- How could you help your grieving friend find a teen support group? Would you be willing to go with him or her? Why or why not?

Internet Sites

Counseling for Loss and Life Changes
www.counselingforloss.com
Links to other grief-related Internet sites

Death and Dying
www.death-dying.com/teen.html
Articles and a special chat room for teens

Hospice Net
www.hospicenet.org
Helping teens cope with grief due to life-threatening illnesses

SA\VE Suicide Awareness Voices of Education
www.save.org
Online grief and outreach support group for survivors of suicide and others

Hot Lines

National AIDS Hot Line
1-800-342-AIDS (1-800-342-2437)

Youth Crisis Hot line
1-800-HIT-HOME (1-800-448-4663)

Useful Addresses

Association for Death Education and
Counseling (ADEC)
638 Prospect Avenue
Hartford, CT 06105-4298
www.adec.org
Promotes information on death education and
makes referrals

Canadian Mental Health Association
2160 Yonge Street
Third Floor
Toronto, ON M4S 2Z3
CANADA
www.cmha.ca/english/homeng.htm
Makes referrals for all types of bereavements

The Compassionate Friends
PO Box 3696
Oak Brook, IL 60522-3696
www.compassionatefriends.org
International self-help group with many
publications on bereavement

National Funeral Directors Association
Washington DC Office
400 C Street Northeast
Washington, DC 20002
www.nfda.org
Provides information on all forms of
bereavement, funerals, and various ways to
handle bodies, such as burial or cremation

National Hospice and Palliative Care
Organization
1700 Diagonal Road, Suite 300
Alexandria, VA 22314
www.nho.org
Provides names of hospices and related service
organizations in different areas

Teen Age Grief (TAG)
PO Box 220034
Newhall, CA 91322-0034
www.smartlink.net/~tag/info.html
Articles about grieving and teenagers; provides
links to other sites

For Further Reading

Davies, Phyllis. *Grief: Climb Toward Understanding.* (5th edition.) San Luis
Obispo, CA: Sunnybank, 1998.

Hawes, Louise. *Rosey in the Present Tense.* New York: Walker, 1999.

Kuehn, Eileen. *Loss: Understanding the Emptiness.* Mankato, MN:
Capstone, 2001.

Peacock, Judith. *Depression.* Mankato, MN: Capstone, 2000.

Rottman, S. L. *Rough Waters.* Atlanta: Peachtree, 1997.

Glossary

bereavement (bi-REEV-muhnt)—the feelings of shock when a loved one dies

denial (di-NYE-uhl)—not wanting to think about death or refusing to accept that a person has died

emotional anesthesia (i-MOH-shuhn-uhl an-iss-THEE-zhuh)—a condition where the emotions feel paralyzed

grieving (GREEV-ing)—a process of dealing with the deep sorrow of a loss

hearse (HURSS)—a vehicle for carrying a dead body to a place of burial

home health aide (HOME HELTH AID)—a person trained to care for the sick at home; home health aides may help patients who receive hospice care.

hospice (HOSS-puhss)—a place where dying people can comfortably spend the last days of their life; a hospice may be in a home or a special building.

interment (in-TUR-muhnt)—the act or ceremony of burying a dead body

living will (LIV-ing WIL)—a legal document that says what treatment a person wants or doesn't want if terminally ill

memento (muh-MEN-toh)—a small gift or token that has a special meaning; sometimes a person puts a memento in the burial casket.

religious tradition (ri-LIJ-uhss truh-DISH-uhn)—religious actions, beliefs, customs, and ceremonies that have been handed down over time

shiva (SHIV-uh)—a time for several days after the burial of a Jewish person when a rabbi reads special prayers; food and refreshments are served, and people visit and remember the life of the deceased.

suicide (SOO-uh-side)—intentional taking of one's own life, or killing oneself

support group (suh-PORT GROOP)—a group of people who meet together to help each other with grief

terminally ill (TUR-muh-nuh-lee IL)—having an illness that can only result in death

Index

active listening, 39, 55, 57–58
Alaskan native peoples, 12
American Indians, 38
anchoring joy, 35, 36
ashes, 8–9
avoidance, 26, 27, 28, 50

blame, 25, 26, 54, 56
body language, 19
burial, 7, 8, 10, 12, 34
    preparing a body for, 7–8, 10

casket, 8, 10, 12–13, 34
celebrating life, 11
cemetery, 10
changing outlook on death, 6, 11
clothing, 21
coffin. *See* casket
confrontation, 26, 29
contracts, 35
coping, 22, 29, 50, 54. *See also*
    grieving process
counselors, 21, 39, 50, 54, 56
cremation, 7, 8–9, 34
crying, 28, 29, 34
cultural practices, 8, 10, 12–13, 21, 38

death
    accepting, 10, 15, 20, 21, 29, 30,
        50
    anticipated, 6–7, 15, 25, 26
    and arts, 9, 19–20, 37, 38
    changing outlook on, 6, 11
    preparing for, 6–7, 15–17, 26
    seriousness of, 11
    sudden, 5, 7, 15, 25, 26, 28, 34, 45,
        54

    violent, 25
    what to expect, 6–7
"Death in the Sick Chamber," 19–20
denial, 6, 27, 47, 58
depression, 49–50

embalming, 8
emotional anesthesia, 27. *See also*
    grieving process, avoidance
empathy, 57

feasts, 12
feelings. *See also* grief work
    anger, 6, 18, 19, 25, 28, 29, 36, 37,
        43, 58
    bereavement, 20
    confusion, 18, 27, 29
    disbelief, 27, 28
    expressing, 19–20, 26, 28, 34, 35,
        37
    fear, 36
    grief, 19, 22, 25–31, 35, 43
    guilt, 18, 25, 26, 28, 30
    numbness, 18, 27, 45, 54
    pain, 18, 21, 28, 34, 48
    relief, 18
    rush of, 18, 19–20
    sadness, 16, 20, 22, 28, 29, 31, 33,
        36, 43
    self-blame, 25, 54, 56
    shock, 20, 26, 27, 28
funeral homes, 7, 34
funeral procession, 10, 11
    wailing, 12
funerals, 8–9, 10, 19, 21, 28, 29, 34,
    54
    planning, 11
    and various customs, 12–13, 21

Index

good-bye, saying, 8, 10–11, 12, 15, 19, 26, 48
    through art and music, 9, 19–20
grief work, 35–38, 59
grieving process, 10, 13, 20, 21, 25–31, 43–44, 45, 53, 54–55. *See also* grief work
    accommodation, 26, 30, 31, 47
    avoidance, 26, 27–28, 50
    confrontation, 26, 29
    growing as a person, 31
    helpful, 33–38, 48
    helping a friend through, 53–59
    organizations, 40, 41, 58
    phases, 26–31, 50, 51
    unhelpful, 47, 48–50

Hawaiians, 12
healing, 21, 22, 26, 27, 33–41
hearse, 10
help, getting, 38–40, 41, 45, 46. *See also* counselors; organizations
home health aides, 16–17
hospice, 16–17, 19
hospitals, 5–6

interment, 7–8, 10
Internet, 40
Islam, 12

Jewish people, 13
journals, 36, 38, 57

letting go, 36, 44, 47–48
lifestyles, healthy, 6
listening, 55, 57–58
lists, 35, 36

living will, 17

machines, 6, 17
mind-mapping, 35, 37
mourning, 21
moving on, 43, 44, 46
Munch, Edvard, 19–20

Native Americans, 38
nurses, 16–17

organizations, 40, 41, 58

processions, 10, 11

relearning life, 30–31, 46–51
religious practices, 8, 12–13, 21

shroud, 8, 12
sitting shiva, 13
suicide, 7, 25, 54. *See also* death, sudden
support groups, 58

talking, 27, 28, 54, 55, 56, 57
technology, medical, 6, 7, 17
terminally ill people, 6, 11, 15, 16–17

ululation, 12
urn, 8–9

wailing, 12
wake, 10
writing, 35, 36, 57